BRIAN HOLZAPFEL

Nerdy Nuggets

A Fun Compilation of Curiosities From the World of Computing

First edition

This book was professionally typeset on Reedsy.
Find out more at reedsy.com

Contents

Introduction

I n the ever-evolving landscape of technology, the world of IT and computers is a realm of constant innovation, discovery, and occasionally, delightful quirkiness. We invite you to explore the fascinating tapestry of facts, anecdotes, and revelations that make the world of IT a captivating and often humorous frontier.

Discovering the humor in the term "bug," as a literal moth caused a malfunction in the Harvard Mark II computer, giving rise to a term now synonymous with computer glitches. Venture into the virtual realm with the story of the first-ever domain name, symbolics.com, registered in 1985. Witness the birth of the World Wide Web, conceived by Sir Tim Berners-Lee in the corridors of CERN. As we navigate through the development of programming languages and the evolution of software, you'll encounter the whimsical origins of Python, named after the comedy group Monty Python.

The world of the internet, a global phenomenon that has connected billions, has its share of intriguing facts. Discover the legend of the "Trojan Room Coffee Pot" webcam, capturing the mundane yet endearing image of a coffee pot at the University of Cambridge.

From the fastest internet speeds to the quirks of programming culture,

"Nerdy Nuggets" takes you on a rollercoaster ride through the often over-looked, quirky, and downright amusing facets of the IT and computer landscape. Whether you are a seasoned tech enthusiast, a curious mind, or someone new to navigating the digital world, this book promises a blend of entertainment and enlightenment.

So, fasten your seatbelts, dear reader, as we embark on this journey through the labyrinth of IT marvels – where every byte tells a story, and every line of code holds a secret waiting to be uncovered. Welcome to the byte-sized wonders that make the world of IT an endlessly fascinating and entertaining domain.

Fantastic Firsts

Welcome to the section of our book titled "Fantastic Firsts," where we embark on a journey through the pioneering moments that have shaped the landscape of information technology and computers. In this chapter, we delve into the remarkable breakthroughs and ingenious inventions that marked the dawn of a new era, transforming the way we interact with technology.

These "Fantastic Firsts" are some of the milestones that laid the groundwork for the digital age, unveiling the stories behind the inaugural moments that shaped our technological landscape. From the first-ever computer mouse to the inception of the World Wide Web, each entry in this section encapsulates the spirit of innovation, curiosity, and the relentless pursuit of pushing boundaries.

Join us as we rewind the clock to witness the birth of the digital revolution, exploring the fascinating tales of the trailblazers who dared to dream beyond the confines of conventional thinking. These stories not only narrate the feats of engineers, programmers, and visionaries but also illuminate the spirit of discovery that continues to drive the evolution of technology.

As we navigate through these "Fantastic Firsts," prepare to be captivated by the tales of ingenious inventions, audacious experiments, and ground-breaking discoveries that have paved the way for the digital wonders we now take for granted. It's a celebration of those pivotal moments that forever altered the trajectory of computing, leaving an indelible mark on the world we inhabit today. So, fasten your seatbelts as we embark on this riveting exploration of the extraordinary beginnings that set the stage for the extraordinary world of IT and computers.

Bug in the Machine

The story of the moth causing a malfunction in the Harvard Mark II computer is a famous incident in the history of computing and is often cited as the origin of the term "bug" in the context of computer science. The event occurred in September 1947 at Harvard University when operators found a moth stuck in one of the relays of the Harvard Mark II computer.

Grace Hopper, a computer scientist and naval officer who was working on the Harvard Mark II at the time, documented the incident in the computer's logbook. The entry reads:

"First actual case of bug being found."

Hopper taped the moth to the logbook and wrote, "Relay #70 Panel F (moth) in the relay." This moment is often considered the first recorded instance of an actual bug causing a computer malfunction.

While the term "bug" had been used in engineering contexts before this incident to refer to glitches or defects, this particular case popularized the use of the term in the context of computer science. The practice of debugging, or finding and fixing errors in computer code, can be traced back to this historical incident involving a literal bug in a computer.

The Birth of the WWW

In the early days of the internet, amidst the humming servers of CERN in 1991, a digital milestone quietly unfolded. Tim Berners-Lee, a scientist at CERN, implemented the first website, and its unassuming URL was "info.cern.ch."

This inaugural website wasn't a dazzling showcase; rather, it served a pragmatic purpose. info.cern.ch wasn't designed to sell products or entertain users; instead, it acted as an informational hub about the World Wide Web project itself. The page provided details on how to create web pages, use browsers, and explained the fundamental concepts of this burgeoning technology.

Imagine a webpage with a plain background, minimal graphics, and a straightforward layout. The first HTML page was, in essence, a set of instructions and information designed to assist fellow researchers and collaborators at CERN. It wasn't adorned with multimedia or flashy elements but embodied the utilitarian spirit of the early web.

The URL info.cern.ch represented a digital handbook, a guidebook for those venturing into the uncharted territory of the World Wide Web. It was an unpretentious start to what would become a vast, interconnected digital landscape.

In the simplicity of its design and purpose, info.cern.ch set the stage for the web's evolution. This unassuming webpage laid the groundwork for the information-sharing powerhouse that the internet has become. The birth of this modest site marked the inception of the global web, where the exchange of knowledge would become more accessible and interconnected than ever before.

Wooden Mouse

In the mid-1960s, amidst the whirring mainframes and punch card routines of early computing, a maverick engineer named Douglas Engelbart embarked on a mission to transform the way humans interacted with computers. His brainchild? The world's first computer mouse – a peculiar wooden contraption with two perpendicular wheels that defied the conventional norms of input devices.

In 1964, Engelbart's wooden prototype, aptly named the "mouse" for its tail-like cord, emerged at the Stanford Research Institute. Unveiling this unconventional creation in 1968 at the Fall Joint Computer Conference in San Francisco, Engelbart delivered what would be known as "The Mother of All Demos." The mouse, along with a suite of groundbreaking technologies like hypertext and collaborative editing, took center stage.

Imagine the scene: an audience accustomed to punch cards and command-line interfaces witnessing Engelbart manipulating a screen cursor with a handheld device. As he deftly moved the mouse, a new era in human-computer interaction unfolded. The mouse, with its humble beginnings in a wooden block, became a symbol of innovation.

Though initially met with skepticism, Engelbart's visionary invention paved the way for the graphical user interfaces of the future. The mouse, evolving from wood to ball-based mechanisms and eventually optical sensors, achieved ubiquity. Engelbart's legacy lives on in every click and scroll, reminding us that even the most unconventional ideas can revolutionize the digital landscape.

The Beginning of E-Commerce

In the early days of the Internet, when the concept of online transactions was in its infancy, a historic event unfolded that marked the birth of e-commerce. On a seemingly ordinary day in August 1994, a man named Dan Kohn made a purchase that would go down in history as the first-ever online retail transaction.

The setting was NetMarket, one of the pioneering online marketplaces. Dan, a music enthusiast, navigated the virtual aisles and stumbled upon an album that caught his interest – Sting's "Ten Summoner's Tales." Seizing the opportunity to be part of a revolutionary moment, he clicked the "Buy" button and entered his payment information.

Little did Dan Kohn know that this seemingly mundane act would become a watershed moment in the evolution of commerce. The transaction, involving a credit card and the secure transmission of data over the internet, set a precedent for a new era of buying and selling.

The significance of this moment was not lost on those who witnessed it. It was a glimpse into the future, a future where physical distance would no longer be a barrier to commerce. The virtual shopping cart and checkout process had taken their first steps, paving the way for the bustling e-commerce landscape we know today.

Dan Kohn's purchase of "Ten Summoner's Tales" may have seemed like just another transaction at the time, but its ripple effect was profound. It heralded an era where the click of a mouse would carry the weight of commerce, where virtual storefronts would replace brick-and-mortar shops, and where the concept of buying and selling would be forever altered by the limitless potential of the online marketplace. In that single transaction, a digital revolution was born, and the landscape of commerce was forever changed.

The Watchful Eye

In the early days of the internet, when the World Wide Web was still finding its virtual feet, a whimsical experiment unfolded at the University of Cambridge that would leave an indelible mark on the digital landscape. The year was 1991, and a group of researchers at the Computer Laboratory, led by Quentin Stafford-Fraser and Paul Jardetzky, concocted an amusing solution to a common office woe – the uncertainty of whether there was fresh coffee in the break room.

Enter the "Trojan Room Coffee Pot Webcam," a humble camera pointed at the department's coffee pot. The live video feed was made accessible to anyone with internet access. With a simple click, users could check the status of the coffee pot from the comfort of their desks.

This seemingly trivial innovation, born out of a desire to solve a mundane problem, became an internet sensation. The webcam, operating on a local network, allowed the global online community a voyeuristic peek into the daily rituals of academia. It wasn't just about coffee; it was about the convergence of technology and humor.

The Trojan Room Coffee Pot Webcam achieved legendary status, and its impact reached far beyond its original purpose. It was a lighthearted reminder that even in the realm of complex technology, there's room for whimsy. Today, as we navigate a world saturated with webcams, this quirky experiment remains a charming testament to the delightful and unexpected intersections of innovation and everyday life.

First Registered Domain

In the early days of the Internet, the digital landscape was a vast, uncharted territory waiting to be explored. Amidst this frontier, the concept of domain names emerged, providing a structured way to navigate the growing web. The first registered domain, a historical marker in the virtual domain of cyberspace, holds a tale of foresight and digital pioneering.

On March 15, 1985, the inaugural domain name to be officially registered was "symbolics.com." Symbolics, Inc., a computer manufacturer based in Cambridge, Massachusetts, staked its claim as the first entity to enter the domain registration arena. Little did they know that this seemingly ordinary act would lay the foundation for the domain-centric internet we know today.

The registration of "symbolics.com" marked a pivotal moment in internet history, signifying the dawn of a new era where businesses, organizations, and individuals could stake their claim in the virtual realm. This seemingly innocuous event paved the way for the explosive growth of domain registrations that followed.

While the digital landscape has evolved exponentially since the registration of the first domain, "symbolics.com" remains a symbolic artifact, a digital monument that heralded the beginning of the structured and navigable internet. The significance of this milestone is not lost in the annals of cyberspace, as it serves as a testament to the visionary spirit that propelled the internet into the interconnected global network we rely on today.

The First Digital Pathfinder

In the early days of the internet, navigating the vast expanse of information was akin to embarking on a treasure hunt without a map. This changed with the advent of the world's first search engine, a digital trailblazer that would transform the way we explore the virtual realm.

Picture the year 1990, a time when the internet was still in its nascent stage. Amidst this digital wilderness, Alan Emtage, a student at McGill University in Montreal, embarked on a mission to create a tool that could help users find specific files on the FTP (File Transfer Protocol) servers scattered across the internet.

With ingenuity and determination, Emtage developed Archie, the pioneering search engine. Unlike the sophisticated algorithms we know today, Archie operated on a simpler premise. It created an index of file names from FTP servers, allowing users to query this index for specific files.

The impact was revolutionary. For the first time, users could systematically search for files rather than blindly navigating directories. Archie became the internet's first digital pathfinder, illuminating the way through the previously uncharted expanses of cyberspace.

The name "Archie" may not resonate as loudly as today's search giants, but its significance is profound. In its humble beginnings, Archie set the stage for the evolution of search engines, paving the way for the sophisticated algorithms and intelligent indexing that power our digital quests today. Alan Emtage's creation marked a pivotal moment in the history of information retrieval, turning the chaotic digital landscape into a navigable terrain, where the thirst for knowledge could be quenched with the stroke of a keyboard. The journey of discovery had found its guide, and the era of search engines had dawned.

Cool Curiosities

Embark on a journey through the vibrant tapestry of "Cool Curiosities" This section is a curated collection of the unexpected, the amusing, and the downright quirky facets that make the world of information technology a playground of delightful surprises. Here, we invite you to explore the lesser-known gems and offbeat anecdotes that add a touch of enchantment to the vast landscape of computers and the internet.

Imagine stumbling upon a tale of a Scandinavian king lending his name to a wireless technology standard or the origin of a programming language named after a British comedy group. These cool curiosities offer a respite from the routine and invite you to marvel at the intriguing stories that often go unnoticed in the grand narrative of IT history.

From the humble beginnings of the keyboard layout that we all know so well to the interesting ways your body is affected by the digital glow, we delve into the playful and unexpected. This section is not just about facts; it's a celebration of the whimsy woven into the fabric of technology.

So, as you turn the pages of "Cool Curiosities," anticipate a delightful exploration where randomness takes center stage, and every fact is a charming revelation. These stories are more than mere footnotes; they are the cool curiosities that inject a sense of wonder into the realm of IT, proving that, beyond the lines of code and circuitry, there's a playful and captivating side to the world of computers and the internet. Welcome to a curated odyssey where every tidbit promises to be as surprising as it is entertaining.

Blinking in the Digital Glow

In the realm where humans and technology intertwine, a peculiar dance emerges when fingers meet keyboards and screens illuminate. It's the ballet of blinking, a subtle shift in rhythm observed in the digital embrace.

Research unveils that the average person blinks 15 to 20 times per minute in regular circumstances. Yet, as eyes fixate on the luminous computer screen, a curious transformation takes place. The blink rate, akin to a metronome adjusting to a novel beat, slows down. The gaze, captivated by the digital glow, hesitates to disrupt the visual enchantment cast by the computer.

The scientific explanation is rooted in the cognitive phenomenon known as "computer vision syndrome." The mesmerizing glow of the screen, combined with the continuous demand for attention and focus, conspires to delay the instinctive act of blinking. Blinking, a natural reflex designed to moisturize and protect the eyes, becomes a casualty in the pursuit of digital immersion.

As users delve into the digital labyrinth, the blinking rhythm persists—a whimsical reminder of the harmonious relationship between humans and their technological counterparts.

The Enchanting Tale of Bluetooth

The name "Bluetooth" carries a whimsical tale that traces its roots to Nordic folklore. Venture back to the 10th century, where the story of a Danish king named Harald "Bluetooth" Gormsson unfolds.

King Harald, known for uniting tribes and fostering peace, became a symbol of unity in Scandinavia. Fast forward to the late 20th century when a group of technology visionaries sought a unifying standard for wireless communication. Inspired by King Harald's legacy of connectivity, the term "Bluetooth" emerged.

The story goes that in the 1990s, as the technology consortium searched for a name for their wireless communication standard, Jim Kardach, an Intel engineer, proposed "Bluetooth" as a code name. Kardach was reading a historical novel about Vikings and their legendary king at the time. King Harald Bluetooth, known for his ability to bring people together, seemed a fitting metaphor for a technology designed to unite various devices seamlessly.

The Bluetooth logo, a combination of Nordic runes representing the initials of King Harald Bluetooth, further solidified the connection between ancient history and modern technology. The symbol beautifully encapsulates the spirit of interoperability and harmony that Bluetooth technology strives to achieve.

So, the next time you pair your smartphone with wireless earbuds or connect devices effortlessly, remember that the term "Bluetooth" echoes not only with signals but also with the ancient tales of a wise and unifying king from the pages of Nordic lore. In the realm of wireless communication, the echoes of King Harald's legacy continue to whisper in the digital airwaves.

Guardians of the Gate

In the vast expanse of the digital realm, where bots and automated scripts lurked in the shadows, a humble word emerged to stand as the sentinel at the gates of cyberspace – "Captcha." The term, a blend of artful design and security ingenuity, traces its origins to a clever play on words.

In the early 2000s, computer scientists Luis von Ahn, Manuel Blum, Nicholas J. Hopper, and John Langford were faced with a challenge: how to distinguish between humans and automated programs in the digital landscape. Seeking a term that encapsulated the essence of their invention, they coined "Captcha," an acronym for "Completely Automated Public Turing test to tell Computers and Humans Apart."

The genius of Captcha lay in its dual purpose. Not only did it serve as a guardian against automated bots attempting to infiltrate online spaces, but it also played a role in digitizing books. Users, unwittingly enlisted as digital archivists, were presented with distorted characters that machines struggled to decipher. By proving they were human through successful Captcha completion, individuals unwittingly contributed to the digitization of texts.

So, every time you decipher those twisted letters or click on the elusive checkbox, remember that you are part of a grand tradition – a tradition born out of the need to secure the digital world and preserve the written word. The term "Captcha" not only guards our online sanctuaries but stands as a testament to the creative spirit that turns challenges into opportunities in the ever-evolving landscape of the internet.

QWERTY Quest

In the rhythmic dance of fingertips on a keyboard, the QWERTY layout orchestrates our digital symphony, but its composition began as an ingenious solution to a mechanical puzzle.

In the late 19th century, Christopher Latham Sholes, a newspaper editor and printer, found himself grappling with the limitations of early typewriters. As typists became faster, the mechanical arms that imprinted ink on paper often jammed, causing frustrating delays.

To address this issue, Sholes devised a layout that intentionally slowed typists down. Collaborating with Samuel Soule and James Densmore, Sholes rearrange the keys, placing commonly used letters farther apart to reduce the likelihood of jams. The result was the QWERTY keyboard, named after the first six letters in the top row.

The QWERTY layout made its debut with the Sholes and Glidden type-writer in 1873, later marketed by E. Remington and Sons. Despite initial skepticism and alternatives proposed by competitors, the QWERTY layout prevailed and became the standard.

As the typewriter gained popularity, the QWERTY layout became deeply ingrained in our typing culture. Its endurance persisted through the transition from typewriters to computer keyboards, maintaining a legacy that echoes through every email, document, and piece of code typed today.

Watcher of the Wiki

Watching over Wikipedia, where knowledge thrives through collabora-tive contributions, a silent guardian protects the integrity of information.

This unsung hero, aptly named the "Wikipedia Vandalism Detection Program," embarked on a mission to uphold the sanctity of the world's largest online encyclopedia.

Picture this: a bustling digital landscape where millions contribute their insights and expertise. In the midst of this collaborative tapestry, the Vandalism Detection Program acts as a watchful sentinel. Its algorithms tirelessly scan the endless edits, sifting through the virtual ink to identify any traces of mischief or misinformation.

The program's journey began as a response to the challenges posed by individuals with less-than-honorable intentions, seeking to distort facts or inject false narratives into the vast reservoir of knowledge. With an arsenal of pattern recognition and linguistic analysis, this digital guardian distinguishes between constructive edits and subtle acts of vandalism.

The importance of the Vandalism Detection Program becomes evident in the delicate dance between freedom of contribution and the need for accuracy. Its algorithms, fueled by the collective commitment to truth, swiftly identify and revert edits that deviate from Wikipedia's ethos of providing reliable, unbiased information.

As Wikipedia continues to evolve, so does the Vandalism Detection Program. It stands as a testament to the collaborative spirit of the online community, a shield against the chaos that misinformation can sow. In the ever-expanding digital library, this guardian silently works, ensuring that the pages of knowledge remain unblemished by the hands of vandals.

Comedy Connection

In the realm of programming languages, few names are as whimsical and serendipitous as "Python." Guido van Rossum, the creator of Python, envisioned a language that was not only powerful but also user-friendly, inspiring a sense of humor and camaraderie among its users. The origin of the name traces back to Guido's fondness for a certain British comedy group—Monty Python's Flying Circus.

In the late 1980s, as Guido van Rossum was developing the language, he sought a name that was short, unique, and a bit quirky. Monty Python's irreverent and clever humor appealed to him, and the name "Python" resonated as a playful choice for his programming language. Guido wanted to inject a sense of fun into the often dry and technical world of programming.

The decision to name the language after Monty Python was more than just a nod to British humor; it reflected Guido's desire to create a language that was enjoyable for developers to use. He aimed to foster a community with a light-hearted and inclusive atmosphere, where users could focus on the joy of programming rather than being bogged down by unnecessary complexities.

The whimsy of the Python name has since become an integral part of the language's identity. Python has grown into one of the most popular and widely used programming languages, and its name serves as a reminder that, in the world of technology, a touch of humor can go a long way in making the learning and development experience both effective and enjoyable.

Magnificent Myths

tep into the realm of "Magnificent Myths" as we unravel the enchanting stories and intriguing legends that have woven themselves into the fabric of IT history. In this section, we embark on a journey through the captivating world of myths – those captivating narratives that, while not grounded in reality, add a layer of mystique to the technological landscape.

Imagine diving into the myth of the origin of the 404 error or uncovering what Wi-Fi actually stands for. These magnificent myths aren't just stories; they are the folklore of the digital age, offering a unique perspective on how the world perceives and interprets the complexities of information technology.

From the fabled invincibility of Mac computers to the false sense of security brought on by incognito mode, each myth holds a nugget of truth or a kernel of humor that has contributed to the colorful tapestry of IT culture.

As you navigate through "Magnificent Myths," anticipate a captivating journey where reality and fiction dance in harmony. These myths, while not factual, play an integral role in shaping perceptions, sparking conversations, and adding a touch of magic to the world of computers and the internet.

So, buckle up for an exploration that transcends the boundaries of truth and fiction, where magnificent myths unfold, inviting you to marvel at the fantastical tales that have become an integral part of the lore surrounding IT. Welcome to a world where the lines between reality and imagination blur, and the myths of technology take center stage.

A Name Without Strings Attached

In the grand overture of technological acronyms, one stands out for its enigmatic simplicity – Wi-Fi. Surprisingly, this ubiquitous term doesn't stand for anything. It's not an acronym for "Wireless Fidelity" as many might assume. Instead, it's a name born out of the desire for a catchy and marketable brand.

The origin of Wi-Fi's nomenclature can be traced back to a brainstorming session led by the founding members of the Wi-Fi Alliance in the late 1990s. Faced with the challenge of branding a new wireless networking technology standard, they sought a name that conveyed the essence of connectivity without the technical jargon.

In a stroke of creative brilliance, the name "Wi-Fi" emerged as a play on the word "Hi-Fi" (High Fidelity), which is often associated with high-quality audio. Wi-Fi, without any predefined meaning, encapsulated the idea of wireless connectivity with a touch of flair. The alliance opted for a name that was easy to remember, marketable, and could transcend linguistic and cultural barriers.

So, next time you connect to Wi-Fi, marvel at the silent symphony of its name – a harmonious blend of simplicity and innovation. Wi-Fi, a term without strings attached, has woven itself into the fabric of our digital lives, a testament to the serendipity that can arise when creativity takes center stage.

Beyond Bars

In the world of mobile connectivity, the presence of signal bars on our devices has become synonymous with the promise of a smooth and swift internet experience. However, the truth behind this common assumption is more nuanced than the number of bars suggests.

The number of signal bars on your device primarily reflects the signal strength between your device and the nearest cell tower. While it's an essential indicator of your connection's stability, it doesn't necessarily correlate with the speed of your internet connection. This misconception often leads users to believe that more bars equate to faster internet speeds.

The reality is that internet speed is influenced by various factors, such as network congestion, the quality of your device, and the capabilities of your service provider. Even with a full set of bars, if the network is congested or your device is outdated, your internet speed may not meet expectations.

Think of signal bars as the signal's highway, not the speed limit. A full set of bars might mean you're on a well-paved road, but the actual speed at which you travel depends on other factors.

To ensure a faster internet experience, users should consider factors like the type of network (3G, 4G, or 5G), the data plan, and the proximity to the nearest cell tower. By understanding that more bars don't necessarily translate to faster internet, users can make informed decisions about optimizing their connectivity and enjoying a smoother online experience.

Room 404: Dispelling the Myth

In the annals of internet lore, the tale of Room 404 has become a digital fable, a story that has woven itself into the fabric of the 404 error's origin. However, as with many legends, the reality behind this narrative diverges from the popular myth.

Contrary to the widely circulated story that Room 404 at CERN served as the birthplace of the 404 error code, the truth is less grandiose. Tim Berners-Lee, the pioneering mind behind the World Wide Web, clarifies that the room number had no intentional connection to the error code.

As we navigate through the corridors of CERN, where the digital pioneers were crafting the foundations of the web. Room 404, often deemed the epicenter of this legendary moment, becomes a mere bystander to the actual genesis of the 404 error.

As the story unfolds, we encounter Tim Berners-Lee and his team grappling with the challenge of managing the growing web. The need for a concise and clear way to signify missing or inaccessible web pages led to the creation of the 404 error code. However, the choice of Room 404 was incidental; it was merely a room where the central hub of the web server was located, devoid of any intentional symbolism. So, while Room 404 at CERN holds its own significance in the history of web development, it was not the mystical birthplace of the 404 error.

Incognito Illusions

In the digital age, the allure of incognito or private browsing mode is shrouded in a myth – the belief that it grants users complete anonymity as they navigate the vast expanses of the internet. However, the reality is far more nuanced, revealing that the cloak of incognito mode doesn't render users invisible to the watchful eyes of the online realm.

The popular misconception is that incognito browsing provides an impenetrable shield against tracking and surveillance. The truth, obscured by the veil of misconception, is that while incognito mode prevents the local browser from storing a browsing history, it does not create an impervious barrier between users and the broader internet landscape.

As we unravel the layers of this myth, we encounter the technical intricacies that challenge the notion of total anonymity. Internet service providers, website operators, and network administrators can still track users' online activities. Additionally, various online platforms employ sophisticated tracking mechanisms that persist even in incognito mode, from personalized ads to website analytics.

This nugget serves as a reminder that while incognito browsing provides a level of privacy by concealing local traces, it falls short of offering foolproof anonymity. Users navigating the internet in incognito mode may find a semblance of discretion, but the myth of total invisibility is dispelled in the face of the intricate web of digital surveillance and tracking technologies that persist beyond the realm of the local browser.

Bandwidth Bogeyman

In the digital realm, a pervasive misconception haunts the corridors of cyberspace—the belief that the internet possesses infinite bandwidth and limitless speed. This anecdote unravels the myth, exposing the reality that, despite the wonders of technology, the internet is not an endless expressway of data.

Let's begin by addressing the common misunderstanding that the internet operates with boundless capacity, akin to an ever-flowing river of information. In truth, the internet's infrastructure has limitations. Bandwidth, the digital highway's capacity, is a finite resource, subject to congestion and fluctuations.

As users traverse the online landscape it is revealed that internet speed is influenced by various factors, including network congestion, the type of connection, and the user's proximity to service infrastructure.

The misconception unfolds like a digital fable, with users often expecting instantaneous access to vast troves of data. The reality, however, is that the Internet operates within the confines of physical infrastructure and technological constraints.

This nugget aims to debunk the notion of infinite internet speed, urging users to understand the limitations and complexities that underpin the digital superhighway. By dispelling the bandwidth bogeyman, it encourages a more nuanced perspective on the capabilities and constraints of the internet, fostering a more realistic understanding of its dynamic nature.

Conclusion

As we reach the final chapter of our exploration into the captivating world of IT, we've unveiled intriguing stories, chuckled at the unexpected humor, and marveled at the innovations that shape our digital landscape.

As we conclude this journey, may your curiosity persist, your code compiles seamlessly, and your digital adventures continue. If this book has brought a smile to your face or sparked your interest, we invite you to share your thoughts. Consider leaving a review and sharing your feedback. Your insights are not just appreciated; they contribute to the topics we explore in the future.

Thank you for joining us on this exploration. Here's to the boundless possibilities of tech, the stories yet to be told, and the laughter that echoes in the digital corridors. Until our paths cross again in the vast realm of IT, happy coding, exploring, and imagining what the future may hold.

BREAKING FREE

A COMPREHENSIVE GUIDE TO QUITTING SMOKING

AUTUMN AVA SMITH

Table of Contents

INTRODUCTION

Hello, I'm your coach .Autumn ava Smith

I'm a passionate advocate for simple living and decluttering. Over the years, I've worked with many clients, helping them to achieve a more organised and peaceful life. Through my experience, I've learned that living with less can bring immense benefits to our mental and emotional well-being, and I'm excited to share my knowledge and expertise with others who are seeking a simpler, more fulfilling lifestyle.

I'm happily married to my wonderful Husband, and we have one delightful child who brings so much joy to our lives. We also have two dogs who keep us on our toes! In my free time, I enjoy reading, and sipping on a cup of my favourite tea, Earl Grey.

I truly believe that a clutter-free home can be a catalyst for positive change, and I'm eager to help others find the peace and contentment that comes with simple living.

Autumn ava Smith

CHAPTER I

Understanding Smoking Addiction

-THE SCIENCE NICOTINE ADDICTION

Certainly! Understanding the science of nicotine addiction is crucial to comprehend why quitting smoking can be challenging and to develop effective strategies to overcome it. Here's an explanation of the science behind nicotine addiction:

Nicotine, a chemical compound found in tobacco products, is the primary addictive substance in cigarettes. When a person smokes a cigarette or uses other tobacco products, nicotine quickly enters the bloodstream through the lungs and reaches the brain within seconds. In the brain, nicotine binds to specific receptors on nerve cells called nicotinic acetylcholine receptors (nAChRs).

Nicotine stimulates the release of several neurotransmitters, including dopamine, which plays a key role in the brain's reward system. Dopamine is associated with feelings of pleasure and reinforces behaviors that lead to its release. When nicotine binds to nAChRs, it triggers the release of dopamine, leading to a pleasurable sensation commonly referred to as a "nicotine rush."

Over time, the brain adapts to the presence of nicotine by reducing the number of available nAChRs and altering the sensitivity of remaining receptors. This process is known as neuroadaptation. As a result, individuals develop a tolerance to nicotine, requiring higher doses to experience the same pleasurable effects. This tolerance contributes to the addictive cycle of smoking.

-THE DANGERS OF SMOKING

Smoking poses significant dangers to both the individual who smokes and those exposed to secondhand smoke. Here are some key dangers associated with smoking:.........

1. Health Risks: Smoking is the leading cause of preventable diseases and premature death worldwide. It dramatically increases the risk of various serious health conditions, including:

CHAPTER 1 CONTINUED

- Lung Cancer: Smoking is the primary cause of lung cancer, responsible for the majority of cases. It damages the cells lining the lungs, leading to the development of cancerous tumors.

- Cardiovascular Disease: Smoking damages blood vessels, increases blood pressure, and promotes the buildup of fatty deposits in arteries. This greatly elevates the risk of heart attacks, strokes, and other cardiovascular diseases.

- Chronic Obstructive Pulmonary Disease (COPD): Smoking is a significant contributor to COPD, a progressive lung disease that includes chronic bronchitis and emphysema. It causes breathing difficulties, chronic coughing, wheezing, and reduced lung function.

- Respiratory Infections: Smoking weakens the immune system and damages the respiratory system, making individuals more susceptible to respiratory infections such as pneumonia, bronchitis, and influenza.

- Increased Cancer Risk: Smoking is linked to various cancers beyond lung cancer, including cancers of the mouth, throat, esophagus, bladder, kidney, pancreas, cervix, and stomach.

- Reduced Fertility and Pregnancy Complications: Smoking can impair fertility in both men and women. Pregnant women who smoke have an increased risk of complications such as ectopic pregnancy, premature birth, low birth weight, and developmental issues in their babies.

- Other Health Issues: Smoking is associated with an increased risk of diabetes, osteoporosis, rheumatoid arthritis, impaired immune function, vision problems, and several other health conditions.

2. Secondhand Smoke: Non-smokers exposed to secondhand smoke are also at risk. Secondhand smoke contains more than 7,000 chemicals, including at least 70 known carcinogens. Breathing in secondhand smoke can lead to respiratory problems, increased risk of heart disease, lung cancer, and other health issues, particularly in children and individuals with pre-existing conditions.

3. Addiction and Dependence: Nicotine, the addictive substance in tobacco, hooks individuals into a cycle of dependence. Nicotine addiction makes it challenging to quit smoking, leading to continued exposure to harmful substances and associated health risks.

4. Financial Burden: Smoking is an expensive habit that can strain individuals' finances. The cost of purchasing cigarettes accumulates over time, creating a significant financial burden and potentially limiting resources for other essential needs.

5. Social and Environmental Impact: Smoking can have negative social consequences, as it is increasingly seen as an undesirable habit. Smoking restrictions in public places and social settings have become more prevalent due to the health risks associated with secondhand smoke.

Understanding the dangers of smoking is essential for individuals to make informed decisions about their health and well-being. Quitting smoking or never starting in the first place is the most effective way to reduce these risks and improve overall health outcomes.

CHAPTER 1 CONTINUED

–WHY QUITTING SMOKING IS IMPORTANT FOR YOUTH

Quitting smoking is particularly important for youth due to the following reasons:

1. Health and Longevity: Smoking poses significant health risks, and quitting at a young age can significantly reduce the likelihood of developing smoking-related diseases later in life. By quitting smoking, young individuals can improve their overall health and increase their life expectancy.

2. Prevention of Addiction: Nicotine addiction can develop quickly, and youth are particularly susceptible to becoming addicted to nicotine. Quitting smoking early prevents the progression of addiction, avoiding the challenges and health consequences associated with long-term nicotine dependence.

3. Brain Development: The adolescent brain is still developing, and nicotine can have detrimental effects on brain structure and function. Smoking during this critical period can impair cognitive abilities, memory, attention, and learning capacity. Quitting smoking allows the brain to recover and develop optimally.

4. Physical Fitness and Athletic Performance: Smoking negatively impacts physical fitness, lung function, and athletic performance. Quitting smoking can enhance lung capacity, stamina, and overall athletic abilities, allowing young individuals to excel in sports and physical activities.

5. Peer Influence and Social Relationships: Youth often face social pressures and influences that may encourage smoking. By quitting smoking, young individuals can serve as positive role models for their peers, promoting healthier choices and influencing their social circles in a positive way.

6. Financial Savings: Smoking is an expensive habit, and quitting at a young age can lead to significant financial savings over time. The money previously spent on cigarettes can be allocated to more productive and enjoyable pursuits, such as education, hobbies, or future goals.

7. Setting Healthy Habits for Life: Quitting smoking early establishes a foundation for a healthier lifestyle. It fosters an awareness of the importance of making positive choices concerning nutrition, exercise, and overall well-being. By quitting smoking, young individuals can build resilience, discipline, and the ability to overcome challenges, which can benefit them in various aspects of life.

8. Environmental Impact: Smoking has negative environmental effects due to the production of cigarette waste and the release of harmful chemicals into the air. By quitting smoking, youth contribute to a cleaner and healthier environment for themselves and future generations.

Quitting smoking at a young age is a powerful investment in one's health, well-being, and future. It empowers youth to take control of their lives, make informed decisions, and pave the way for a healthier, more fulfilling future.

CHAPTER 2

Preparing For Quitting smoking

-ASSESSING YOUR SMOKING HABITS

Assessing your smoking habit is an important step in understanding your relationship with cigarettes and developing a plan to quit. Here are some key steps to assess your smoking habit:

1. Self-Reflection: Take some time to reflect on your smoking habits. Consider the following questions:
   - How long have you been smoking?
   - How frequently do you smoke?
   - How many cigarettes do you typically smoke in a day?
   - When and where do you usually smoke?
   - Are there specific triggers or situations that prompt you to smoke?
   - How do you feel physically and emotionally when you smoke or when you don't smoke?
   - Have you tried to quit smoking in the past? If so, what were the challenges you faced?

2. Keep a Smoking Journal: Start keeping a journal to track your smoking patterns and habits. Note the time, location, and circumstances surrounding each cigarette you smoke. This can help you identify patterns, triggers, and situations where you may be more likely to smoke.

3. Nicotine Dependency Assessment: Assess your level of nicotine dependency to understand the physical aspect of your smoking habit. Consider factors such as:
   - How soon after waking up do you typically smoke your first cigarette?
   - Do you experience cravings and withdrawal symptoms when you try to cut down or abstain from smoking?
   - How difficult do you find it to refrain from smoking in situations where it is not allowed?
   - Have you ever tried nicotine replacement therapy or medications to quit smoking?

4. Health Evaluation: Reflect on your health and any smoking-related symptoms you may be experiencing. Consider:
   - Do you notice any shortness of breath, coughing, or wheezing?
   - Have you noticed changes in your sense of taste or smell?
   - Have you experienced any smoking-related illnesses or health issues?
   - Are you aware of any family history of smoking-related diseases?

5. Emotional and Psychological Assessment: Evaluate the emotional and psychological aspects of your smoking habit. Consider:
   - Do you use smoking as a way to cope with stress, anxiety, or other emotions?
   - Does smoking provide you with a sense of relaxation or comfort?
   - Have you noticed any negative effects of smoking on your mental well-being or self-esteem?

By assessing your smoking habit through self-reflection, journaling, nicotine dependency evaluation, health evaluation, and emotional assessment, you can gain valuable insights into your smoking patterns, triggers, and dependencies. This self-awareness will serve as a foundation for developing a personalized quit plan and implementing effective strategies to quit smoking successfully.

CHAPTER 2 CONTINUED

–SETTING A QUIT DATE

Setting a quit smoking date is an important step in the process of smoking. It involves choosing a specific date on which you commit to stop smoking and begin your journey towards a smoke-free life. Here's an explanation of how to set a quit smoking date effectively:

1. Choose a Meaningful Date: Select a quit smoking date that holds significance for you. It could be a significant milestone like a birthday or anniversary, the start of a new month or year, or any date that resonates with you personally. Having a meaningful date can enhance your motivation and provide a sense of purpose as you embark on your quit journey.

2. Give Yourself Enough Time: It is important to give yourself sufficient time to prepare for your quit smoking date. This allows you to mentally and emotionally prepare for the challenges that may arise, gather resources, and develop coping strategies. Consider giving yourself a few weeks to a month to plan and get ready.

3. Consider Potential Triggers: Reflect on situations, places, or people that might trigger cravings to smoke. Take these triggers into account when selecting your quit date. For example, if you have a social event where smoking is prevalent, it may be wise to choose a quit date after that event to minimize temptation and increase your chances of success.

4. Plan for Support: Inform your friends, family, and support network about your quit smoking date. Seek their support and let them know how they can help you during your quitting process. Having a support system in place can greatly increase your chances of success.

5. Prepare for Nicotine Withdrawal: Nicotine withdrawal symptoms can be challenging to manage, especially in the initial days after quitting. Educate yourself about common withdrawal symptoms and develop a plan to cope with them. Consider talking to your healthcare provider about nicotine replacement therapy (NRT) or other medications that can help ease withdrawal symptoms.

6. Remove Smoking Triggers: Prior to your quit smoking date, remove smoking–related items from your environment. Get rid of cigarettes, lighters, ashtrays, and any other reminders of smoking. Clean your living space to eliminate the smell of smoke and create a fresh environment that supports your smoke-free journey.

7. Mental Preparation: Use the time leading up to your quit date to mentally prepare yourself. Reflect on your reasons for quitting, set clear goals, and visualize yourself as a non-smoker. Develop positive affirmations and motivations to reinforce your commitment to quit smoking.

8. Create a Quit Plan: Develop a personalized quit plan that includes strategies to cope with cravings, stress, and other challenges. Identify alternative activities, such as exercise, hobbies, or deep breathing exercises, to replace the habit of smoking. Explore resources and support programs available to assist you in your quit journey.

Remember, setting a quit smoking date is a powerful commitment to yourself and your health. It marks the beginning of your journey towards a healthier life free from the harms of smoking. Stay motivated, seek support, and be kind to yourself throughout the process.

CHAPTER 2 CONTINUED

–IDENTIFYING TRIGGERS AND PATTERNS

Identifying triggers and patterns of smoking is a crucial step in understanding the factors that contribute to your smoking habit. By recognizing these triggers and patterns, you can develop strategies to effectively manage and overcome them. Here's how to identify triggers and patterns of smoking:

1. Self-Reflection: Take time to reflect on your smoking habits and pay attention to the situations, emotions, or circumstances that typically lead you to smoke. Ask yourself the following questions:
   - When do you usually smoke? Is it in the morning, after meals, during breaks, or in specific social situations?
   - Are there specific places or environments where you tend to smoke more?
   - How do you feel before, during, and after smoking? Are there specific emotions, such as stress, boredom, or social anxiety, that trigger your urge to smoke?

2. Keep a Smoking Journal: Maintain a journal to track your smoking habits and record the details surrounding each cigarette you smoke. Note the time, location, your emotional state, and any specific triggers or events associated with each smoking episode. This journal can help you identify patterns and common themes.

3. Social and Environmental Triggers: Consider the social and environmental factors that may prompt you to smoke. These could include being around friends or colleagues who smoke, being in places where smoking is allowed or encouraged, or engaging in specific activities that are associated with smoking, such as drinking alcohol or having a coffee break.

4. Emotional Triggers: Emotions often play a significant role in smoking habits. Reflect on the emotions or situations that tend to trigger your urge to smoke. Common emotional triggers may include stress, anxiety, sadness, anger, or even positive emotions like celebration or relaxation.

CHAPTER 2 CONTINUED

5. Habits and Routines: Smoking can become intertwined with daily habits and routines. Pay attention to the habits and rituals associated with smoking, such as lighting up after a meal, during a work break, or while driving. These habits can become automatic triggers for smoking.

6. Social and Peer Influence: Assess the influence of friends, family members, or social circles on your smoking habit. Peer pressure and the desire to fit in can be strong triggers for smoking, especially among younger individuals. Evaluate the impact of these social dynamics on your smoking behavior.

7. Physical Dependency: Nicotine addiction creates a physical dependency on cigarettes. The urge to smoke can be heightened by nicotine withdrawal symptoms, such as cravings, irritability, restlessness, or difficulty concentrating. Recognize these physical triggers and patterns that arise due to nicotine dependency.

8. Analyze Your Smoking Journal: Review your smoking journal and look for patterns and trends. Pay attention to common triggers that consistently appear. Look for any connections between specific situations, emotions, or habits and your smoking episodes.

By identifying triggers and patterns of smoking, you gain insight into the specific circumstances and factors that contribute to your smoking habit. This knowledge will help you develop targeted strategies and coping mechanisms to overcome these triggers and successfully navigate the quitting process.

CHAPTER 2 CONTINUED

–BUILDING MOTIVATION AND WILLPOWER

Building motivation and willpower against smoking is crucial for successfully quitting and maintaining a smoke-free life. Here are some strategies to help you strengthen your motivation and willpower:

1. Identify Your Reasons: Clarify why you want to quit smoking and the specific benefits it will bring to your life. Make a list of the reasons that are most meaningful to you, such as improving your health, setting a positive example for loved ones, saving money, or regaining control over your life. Keep this list visible and refer to it regularly to reinforce your motivation.

2. Educate Yourself: Learn about the harmful effects of smoking on your health and the risks associated with tobacco use. Understanding the damage smoking causes to your body, such as increased risk of cancer, heart disease, and respiratory problems, can serve as a powerful motivator. Stay informed about the benefits of quitting and the positive changes that occur in your body after you stop smoking.

3. Set Clear Goals: Establish specific and measurable goals related to quitting smoking. Define your desired quit date, the milestones you want to achieve, and the steps you will take to reach those goals. Breaking down the process into smaller, manageable tasks can make your journey feel more achievable and help you stay focused.

4. Visualize Success: Use the power of visualization to imagine yourself as a non-smoker, enjoying a healthier and smoke-free life. Visualize the positive outcomes and benefits of quitting smoking. Create vivid mental images of yourself engaging in activities you enjoy, free from the constraints and health risks of smoking. This positive visualization can strengthen your motivation and willpower.

CHAPTER 2 CONTINUED

5. Seek Support: Surround yourself with a supportive network of family, friends, or support groups who understand your desire to quit smoking. Share your goals and progress with them, and lean on their encouragement during challenging times. Consider joining smoking cessation programs or seeking professional help to increase your chances of success.

6. Replace Smoking Habits: Develop healthier habits and activities to replace the habit of smoking. Engage in physical exercise, practice deep breathing or relaxation techniques, pursue hobbies, or spend time with non-smoking friends. Occupying your time and mind with positive activities can distract you from cravings and reinforce your willpower.

7. Manage Stress: Stress is a common trigger for smoking. Develop effective stress management techniques, such as regular exercise, meditation, mindfulness, or seeking therapy. By addressing stress in healthy ways, you reduce the likelihood of turning to smoking as a coping mechanism.

8. Celebrate Milestones: Recognize and reward yourself for every milestone achieved during your quitting journey. Celebrate the progress you make, whether it's a day, a week, or a month without smoking. Treat yourself to something meaningful or enjoyable as a reminder of the benefits you're gaining by staying smoke-free.

9. Stay Positive and Persistent: Quitting smoking can be challenging, and setbacks may occur. It's important to stay positive and persistent. If you experience a relapse, don't give up. Learn from the experience, reassess your strategies, and renew your commitment to quitting. Remember that quitting is a process, and each attempt brings you closer to success.

Building motivation and willpower against smoking requires commitment, perseverance, and a positive mindset. By utilizing these strategies and staying focused on your goals, you can strengthen your resolve to quit smoking and create a healthier, smoke-free life for yourself.

CHAPTER 3

Exploring Quitting Methods

-NICOTINE REPLACEMENT THERAPY

Nicotine replacement therapy (NRT) is a widely used method to help people quit smoking by providing a controlled dose of nicotine without the harmful chemicals found in tobacco smoke. It aims to reduce withdrawal symptoms and cravings associated with nicotine addiction, making the quitting process more manageable. Here's an explanation of nicotine replacement therapy:

1. How It Works: NRT works by delivering nicotine to the body through safer alternatives, such as patches, gum, lozenges, inhalers, or nasal sprays. These products contain nicotine in lower and controlled doses compared to cigarettes. By providing a steady supply of nicotine, NRT helps reduce withdrawal symptoms and cravings, making it easier to gradually reduce nicotine dependence.

2. Types of NRT Products:
   a. Nicotine Patch: The patch is a thin, adhesive patch that is applied to the skin, usually on the upper arm or shoulder. It releases a steady amount of nicotine into the bloodstream throughout the day, helping to alleviate cravings and withdrawal symptoms.
   b. Nicotine Gum: Nicotine gum is chewed to release nicotine, which is absorbed through the lining of the mouth. It is available in various strengths and flavors, and the gum is chewed intermittently to manage cravings.
   c. Nicotine Lozenge: The lozenge is a small tablet that dissolves slowly in the mouth, releasing nicotine. It is available in different strengths and flavors, and it can be used as needed to alleviate cravings.
   d. Nicotine Inhaler: The inhaler is a device that delivers nicotine in the form of vapor. It mimics the hand-to-mouth action of smoking and allows users to inhale nicotine vapor through a mouthpiece.
   e. Nicotine Nasal Spray: The nasal spray delivers nicotine through a fine mist sprayed into the nostrils. It provides quick relief from cravings but requires a prescription in many countries.

3. Effectiveness: NRT has been shown to increase the chances of successfully quitting smoking. It helps manage withdrawal symptoms and cravings, making it easier to break the habit of smoking. When used as directed and combined with behavioral support, NRT can double a person's chances of successfully quitting smoking compared to quitting without assistance.

CHAPTER 3 CONTINUED

4. Proper Usage: It is important to follow the instructions provided with each NRT product and consult a healthcare professional for guidance. Different products have specific usage guidelines, such as recommended dosages, duration of use, and instructions for gradually reducing nicotine intake over time.

5. Combination Therapy: Combining different forms of NRT, such as using a patch along with gum or lozenges, can be more effective than using a single NRT product alone. This approach can provide more comprehensive nicotine replacement and address different aspects of nicotine addiction.

6. Potential Side Effects: NRT products are generally safe when used as directed, but they can cause side effects in some individuals. Common side effects include skin irritation from patches, jaw pain or soreness from gum, throat irritation from inhalers, and nasal irritation from nasal sprays. These side effects are usually mild and temporary.

7. Consultation with Healthcare Provider: Before starting NRT, it is recommended to consult with a healthcare provider, especially for individuals with underlying medical conditions or those taking other medications. They can provide personalized guidance, recommend appropriate NRT products, and address any concerns or questions.

Nicotine replacement therapy can be a valuable tool in the quitting process, providing nicotine in a safer form and helping manage withdrawal symptoms and cravings. However, it's important to remember that NRT alone may not address all aspects of smoking addiction, and combining it with behavioral support and lifestyle changes can increase the chances of long-term success in quitting smoking.

CHAPTER 3 CONTINUED

–PRESCRIPTION MEDICATION

There are prescription medications available that can aid in smoking cessation by reducing nicotine cravings and withdrawal symptoms. These medications are typically used under the guidance of a healthcare professional and can significantly increase the chances of successfully quitting smoking. Here's an explanation of some commonly prescribed medications for smoking cessation:

1. Bupropion (Zyban, Wellbutrin): Originally developed as an antidepressant, bupropion has been found to be effective in helping people quit smoking. It works by reducing nicotine cravings and withdrawal symptoms. Bupropion is usually taken for several weeks before the quit date and continued for a prescribed duration afterward. Common side effects may include dry mouth, insomnia, and in rare cases, mood changes or seizures.

2. Varenicline (Chantix): Varenicline is a medication specifically designed to aid smoking cessation. It works by blocking nicotine receptors in the brain, reducing the satisfaction and reward associated with smoking. Varenicline also helps alleviate withdrawal symptoms. It is typically taken for a few weeks before the quit date and continued for a prescribed duration afterward. Common side effects may include nausea, vivid dreams, and changes in taste perception. It is important to monitor mood and seek medical attention if any unusual or severe changes occur.

3. Clonidine: Clonidine is primarily used to treat high blood pressure but has also been found to help with smoking cessation. It can help reduce withdrawal symptoms such as anxiety, irritability, and restlessness. Clonidine is usually administered as a patch or tablet and is used for a limited duration during the quitting process. It may cause side effects such as drowsiness, dry mouth, and low blood pressure.

It's important to note that these medications should be prescribed and monitored by a healthcare professional who can evaluate your medical history, current medications, and any potential contraindications or side effects.

In addition to these medications, behavioral support and counseling are often recommended in conjunction with prescription medications for smoking cessation. Combining medication with counseling or behavioral therapies can enhance the effectiveness of the quitting process and provide comprehensive support.

It is crucial to consult with a healthcare provider to determine the most appropriate medication and treatment plan for your specific needs. They can provide personalized guidance, monitor your progress, and address any questions or concerns you may have.

CHAPTER 3 CONTINUED

–ALTERNATIVE THERAPIES AND TECHNIQUES

In addition to conventional methods like medication and counseling, there are alternative therapies and techniques that some individuals find helpful in quitting smoking. While the effectiveness of these approaches may vary from person to person, they can be worth exploring as complementary strategies. Here are some alternative therapies and techniques commonly used for smoking cessation:

1. Acupuncture: Acupuncture involves the insertion of thin needles into specific points on the body. Some people believe that acupuncture can help reduce cravings and withdrawal symptoms associated with nicotine addiction. While the scientific evidence is mixed, some studies suggest that acupuncture may have a positive impact on smoking cessation by promoting relaxation and reducing anxiety.

2. Hypnotherapy: Hypnotherapy involves guided relaxation and focused attention to achieve a state of heightened suggestibility. During a hypnotherapy session, a trained therapist may use suggestions and imagery to help change attitudes and behaviors related to smoking. Hypnotherapy aims to tap into the subconscious mind, reinforcing the desire to quit smoking and reducing cravings. While research on its effectiveness is limited, some individuals report positive outcomes.

3. Mindfulness and Meditation: Mindfulness and meditation practices can help increase awareness of cravings and develop coping mechanisms to manage them. By learning to observe cravings without judgment and cultivating a sense of present-moment awareness, mindfulness can help individuals better understand their smoking triggers and make conscious choices to resist cravings.

4. Yoga and Exercise: Engaging in physical activity, such as yoga, can provide a distraction from cravings and promote overall well-being. Yoga combines movement, breathing exercises, and mindfulness, which can help reduce stress and increase self-awareness. Regular exercise, whether it's yoga, jogging, or any other form of physical activity, can also help manage cravings, improve mood, and support the quitting process.

5. Herbal Remedies: Some individuals turn to herbal remedies to support their smoking cessation efforts. For example, lobelia (also known as Indian tobacco) has been used traditionally to help reduce nicotine cravings. However, it's essential to exercise caution when using herbal remedies, as their safety and effectiveness may vary. Consult with a healthcare professional before trying any herbal supplements.

6. Support Groups and Online Communities: Joining support groups or online communities can provide a sense of belonging and understanding as you navigate the challenges of quitting smoking. Connecting with others who are going through or have gone through a similar journey can offer valuable advice, encouragement, and accountability.

7. Aromatherapy: Aromatherapy involves the use of essential oils to create specific scents that can help reduce cravings and promote relaxation. Some oils, such as lavender or citrus scents, are believed to have calming effects and may aid in managing stress and cravings associated with smoking.

It's important to note that while these alternative therapies and techniques may be beneficial for some individuals, they should not replace evidence-based approaches like medication and counseling. Quitting smoking is a highly personal journey, and what works for one person may not work for another. It's recommended to consult with a healthcare professional or a qualified practitioner in each respective therapy to determine the most suitable approach for your needs.

CHAPTER 4

Coping With Cravings and Withdrawal Symptoms

1. Cravings: Cravings are intense desires or urges to smoke that can be triggered by various factors such as stress, social situations, or specific cues associated with smoking (e.g., seeing someone else smoke or smelling cigarette smoke). Cravings typically arise due to the physical and psychological dependence on nicotine developed through smoking.

2. Urges: Urges are similar to cravings but may be less intense and more fleeting. They can be sudden and powerful impulses to smoke, often triggered by specific situations or emotions. Urges can last for a short period and can be accompanied by physical sensations or thoughts urging you to smoke.

3. Mindful Awareness: Developing mindful awareness of cravings and urges involves observing them without judgment and accepting them as temporary experiences. Rather than resisting or fighting the cravings, acknowledge them as a normal part of the quitting process. Recognize that cravings and urges will pass over time, typically lasting a few minutes.

4. Distraction Techniques: Engaging in activities that redirect your attention can help manage cravings and urges. Find healthy distractions such as physical exercise, reading a book, listening to music, or engaging in a hobby. The idea is to shift your focus away from smoking-related thoughts and occupy your mind with something else.

5. Deep Breathing and Relaxation: Deep breathing exercises and relaxation techniques can help reduce the intensity of cravings and promote a sense of calm. Practice deep, slow breaths, focusing on the inhalation and exhalation. Utilize relaxation techniques like progressive muscle relaxation or guided imagery to help relax your body and mind during cravings.

6. Behavioral Strategies: Replace the smoking habit with healthier behaviors. For example, instead of reaching for a cigarette, chew sugar-free gum, snack on healthy foods, drink water, or engage in oral substitutes like toothpicks or straws. Modify your routines and habits associated with smoking to disrupt the automatic response of reaching for a cigarette.

7. Support System: Seek support from friends, family, or support groups. Discussing your cravings and urges with others who have gone through or are going through the same process can provide understanding, encouragement, and helpful coping strategies. It's essential to have a support system that can offer guidance and keep you motivated during challenging times.

8. Positive Reinforcement: Remind yourself of the reasons why you want to quit smoking and the benefits you'll experience. Celebrate small victories and milestones along the way. Reward yourself with non-smoking-related treats or activities to reinforce your progress and keep your motivation strong.

Remember, cravings and urges are temporary, and they will gradually decrease in frequency and intensity as you progress on your quitting journey. It's important to have patience, persistence, and a positive mindset. If needed, consider seeking professional help from healthcare providers or smoking cessation programs to receive additional guidance and support tailored to your specific needs..

CHAPTER 5

Nurturing a Healthy Lifestyle

-THE IMPORTANCE OF EXERCISE

Exercise plays a significant role in the process of quitting smoking and maintaining long-term abstinence. Here are some key reasons why exercise is important when quitting smoking:

1. Craving Reduction: Engaging in physical activity can help reduce the intensity and frequency of cravings for cigarettes. Exercise releases endorphins, which are chemicals in the brain that promote feelings of well-being and can help counteract nicotine withdrawal symptoms. When cravings arise, participating in exercise can provide a healthy distraction and help manage the urge to smoke.

2. Stress Reduction: Quitting smoking can be a stressful endeavor, as nicotine withdrawal can lead to increased anxiety and irritability. Exercise is known to be an effective stress reliever, as it promotes the release of neurotransmitters like serotonin and dopamine, which can improve mood and reduce stress. Regular physical activity can help manage the stress associated with quitting smoking and prevent relapse triggered by stressors.

3. Mood Enhancement: Quitting smoking can initially lead to fluctuations in mood as the body adjusts to the absence of nicotine. Exercise has been shown to enhance overall mood and reduce feelings of depression and anxiety. The release of endorphins during exercise can provide a natural mood boost and contribute to a more positive outlook during the quitting process.

4. Weight Management: Weight gain is a common concern for individuals who quit smoking. Nicotine can suppress appetite and boost metabolism, so when you stop smoking, your metabolism may temporarily decrease, and you may experience increased food cravings. Regular exercise can help manage weight gain by burning calories, increasing metabolism, and improving body composition. It can also serve as a healthy outlet for managing emotions and stress instead of turning to food.

5. Health Benefits: Smoking is associated with numerous health risks, including cardiovascular disease, lung disease, and various types of cancer. Engaging in regular exercise can improve cardiovascular health, strengthen lung function, and reduce the risk of developing smoking-related diseases. By quitting smoking and adopting an active lifestyle, you can greatly enhance your overall health and well-being.

6. Healthy Habit Formation: Quitting smoking requires breaking the habit of reaching for a cigarette in various situations. By incorporating exercise into your daily routine, you can establish a new, healthier habit that serves as a positive alternative to smoking. It can provide structure, routine, and a sense of accomplishment as you work towards your fitness goals while staying smoke-free.

When implementing exercise as part of your smoking cessation plan, consider activities that you enjoy and that align with your fitness level. Start gradually and gradually increase intensity and duration over time. Aim for a combination of cardiovascular exercises (e.g., brisk walking, jogging, cycling) and strength training exercises (e.g., weightlifting, bodyweight exercises) to reap the full range of benefits..

CHAPTER 5 CONTINUED

–BALANCE NUTRITION AND HYDRATION

Maintaining balanced nutrition and hydration is essential when quitting smoking, as it can support your overall health, aid in managing withdrawal symptoms, and improve your chances of successfully quitting. Here's an explanation of the importance of balanced nutrition and hydration during the smoking cessation process:

1. Nutrient Support: Quitting smoking can have an impact on your body's nutrient needs. Nicotine, the addictive substance in cigarettes, can suppress appetite and increase metabolism. When you quit smoking, your appetite may increase, and your metabolism may temporarily decrease. It's important to focus on consuming a nutritious, well-balanced diet to provide your body with the essential nutrients it needs during this transition.

2. Managing Cravings and Withdrawal Symptoms: Proper nutrition can help manage cravings and withdrawal symptoms associated with quitting smoking. Including a variety of nutrient-dense foods in your diet, such as fruits, vegetables, whole grains, lean proteins, and healthy fats, can help stabilize blood sugar levels and reduce cravings. Avoiding excessive consumption of sugary foods and caffeine can also help manage cravings and prevent energy crashes.

3. Mood and Energy Levels: Quitting smoking can initially lead to changes in mood and energy levels. Proper nutrition plays a crucial role in supporting stable mood and energy throughout the quitting process. Consuming balanced meals and snacks that include complex carbohydrates, lean proteins, and healthy fats can provide sustained energy and promote stable moods..

CHAPTER 5 CONTINUED

4. Antioxidant Protection: Smoking exposes the body to harmful chemicals and increases oxidative stress, which can damage cells and contribute to various health problems. Consuming a diet rich in antioxidants, such as fruits, vegetables, and whole grains, can help counteract oxidative stress and support overall cellular health. Antioxidants also play a role in reducing inflammation and promoting the body's natural detoxification processes.

5. Hydration: Staying properly hydrated is crucial for overall health and can support your efforts to quit smoking. Drinking an adequate amount of water throughout the day can help flush out toxins, maintain proper bodily functions, and reduce potential side effects of nicotine withdrawal, such as headaches and dry mouth. Aim for at least 8 cups (64 ounces) of water per day, and adjust your intake based on your activity level and individual needs.

6. Oral Fixation Replacement: Smoking often involves the repetitive hand-to-mouth motion, which can become ingrained as a habit. This habit can be substituted with healthier options to reduce the risk of weight gain. For example, instead of reaching for a cigarette, opt for sugar-free gum, carrot sticks, or other low-calorie snacks to satisfy the oral fixation without compromising your overall nutrition and weight management goals.

When focusing on balanced nutrition and hydration during the smoking cessation process, consider the following tips:

- Consume a variety of nutrient-dense foods, including fruits, vegetables, whole grains, lean proteins, and healthy fats.
- Limit your intake of processed foods, sugary snacks, and beverages high in caffeine.
- Stay hydrated by drinking water throughout the day and reduce the consumption of sugary drinks and excessive caffeine.
- Incorporate antioxidant-rich foods into your diet, such as berries, leafy greens, nuts, and seeds.
- Eat regular, balanced meals to stabilize blood sugar levels and manage cravings.
- Consider incorporating vitamin and mineral supplements if needed, but consult with a healthcare professional before doing so.

Remember, a balanced approach to nutrition and hydration is crucial for overall well-being and can support your efforts to quit smoking. If you have specific dietary concerns or medical conditions, it is advisable to consult with a healthcare professional or registered dietitian for personalized guidance

CHAPTER 5 CONTINUED

–SLEEP AND RESTORATIVE PRACTICES

Sleep and restorative practices play a vital role in the process of quitting smoking. Getting sufficient sleep and incorporating restorative activities into your routine can support your efforts to quit smoking by promoting physical and mental well-being. Here's an explanation of the importance of sleep and restorative practices during the smoking cessation process:

1. Nicotine Withdrawal and Sleep Disruption: Nicotine is a stimulant that can interfere with sleep patterns. When you quit smoking, nicotine withdrawal symptoms may arise, including difficulty falling asleep, nighttime awakenings, and restless sleep. These disruptions can lead to sleep deprivation, which can negatively impact your mood, energy levels, and overall well-being. Prioritizing sleep can help minimize withdrawal symptoms and improve your ability to cope with the challenges of quitting smoking.

2. Stress Reduction and Relaxation: Quitting smoking can be a stressful process, as nicotine withdrawal can trigger feelings of anxiety and irritability. Engaging in restorative practices such as relaxation techniques, meditation, deep breathing exercises, or gentle stretching can help reduce stress, promote relaxation, and improve your ability to manage cravings and withdrawal symptoms. These practices can also enhance your overall well-being and support a positive mindset during the quitting process.

3. Improving Mood and Mental Health: Sleep deprivation and nicotine withdrawal can both contribute to changes in mood, increased irritability, and feelings of depression or anxiety. Quality sleep and restorative practices can help regulate emotions, improve mood stability, and support mental well-being. Prioritizing restorative activities can provide a positive outlet for managing emotions and reduce the risk of relapse triggered by negative feelings.

4. Energy Restoration: Quitting smoking can initially lead to decreased energy levels and feelings of fatigue. Engaging in restorative practices, such as taking breaks, napping if needed, or practicing relaxation techniques, can help restore energy levels and combat fatigue. Prioritizing restful activities can provide the necessary rejuvenation for both the body and mind during the quitting process.

5. Establishing Healthy Sleep Habits: Quitting smoking provides an opportunity to establish healthy sleep habits. Maintain a consistent sleep schedule by going to bed and waking up at the same time each day. Create a relaxing bedtime routine that promotes sleep, such as avoiding stimulating activities before bed, keeping your bedroom environment conducive to sleep (cool, dark, and quiet), and engaging in relaxation techniques. These habits can help improve the quality and duration of your sleep, supporting the overall quitting process.

6. Self-Care and Stress Management: Quitting smoking requires self-care and stress management. Engaging in restorative practices is a form of self-care that can help you navigate the challenges of quitting. Prioritize activities that promote relaxation and rejuvenation, such as taking warm baths, practicing mindfulness, journaling, or engaging in activities you find enjoyable and fulfilling. These practices can help reduce stress, improve your overall well-being, and provide healthy alternatives to smoking for coping with stress.

7. Cognitive Function and Focus: Quality sleep and restorative practices contribute to improved cognitive function, including attention, concentration, and memory. Quitting smoking can initially lead to cognitive challenges as your body adjusts to nicotine withdrawal. Prioritizing sleep and engaging in restorative activities can enhance brain function, support mental clarity, and improve your ability to stay focused and committed to your quit smoking goals.

Remember, everyone's sleep needs and restorative practices can vary. Listen to your body and prioritize activities that work best for you. If you continue to experience sleep disturbances or significant difficulties with mood or mental health, consider seeking guidance from a healthcare professional who can provide personalized advice and support.

By incorporating adequate sleep and restorative practices into your quitting journey, you can enhance your overall well-being, manage withdrawal symptoms, reduce stress, and increase your chances of successfully quitting smoking..

CHAPTER 6

Celebrating Success: Life After Smoking

-REAPING THE BENEFITS OF QUITTING

Quitting smoking brings numerous benefits that positively impact both your short-term and long-term health. Here are some of the key benefits you can expect to reap when you quit smoking:

1. Improved Respiratory Health: Smoking damages the lungs and can lead to various respiratory issues such as chronic cough, wheezing, and shortness of breath. When you quit smoking, your lung function starts to improve, and over time, your risk of developing lung diseases like chronic bronchitis and emphysema decreases. You'll experience easier breathing, increased lung capacity, and a reduced risk of respiratory infections.

2. Cardiovascular Health Improvement: Smoking is a major risk factor for cardiovascular diseases such as heart attacks, strokes, and peripheral artery disease. When you quit smoking, your cardiovascular system begins to repair itself. Within a few months, your blood pressure and heart rate start to decrease, and your circulation improves. Over time, your risk of heart disease decreases significantly, leading to a healthier heart and blood vessels.

3. Reduced Cancer Risk: Smoking is the leading cause of various types of cancer, including lung, throat, mouth, esophageal, pancreatic, bladder, kidney, and cervical cancer. By quitting smoking, you significantly lower your risk of developing these cancers. Your body's ability to repair damaged DNA improves, and the risk continues to decrease the longer you stay smoke-free.

4. Enhanced Taste and Smell: Smoking dulls the senses of taste and smell. When you quit smoking, your taste buds and olfactory receptors begin to heal, leading to an improved ability to taste and smell things more vividly. Food will become more enjoyable, and you'll be able to appreciate the aromas in your environment.

CHAPTER 6 CONTINUED

5. Improved Skin Health: Smoking accelerates the aging process and contributes to premature wrinkles, dull skin, and a sallow complexion. When you quit smoking, your skin receives better oxygen and nutrients, leading to improved skin health. Over time, you may notice a reduction in wrinkles, improved skin tone, and a healthier, more youthful appearance.

6. Better Oral Health: Smoking is detrimental to oral health, causing issues such as bad breath, yellowed teeth, gum disease, and tooth loss. When you quit smoking, your oral health starts to improve. Your breath becomes fresher, teeth become whiter, and your risk of gum disease decreases. Quitting smoking also reduces the risk of oral cancers.

7. Increased Energy and Fitness Levels: Smoking affects your overall energy levels and physical fitness. When you quit smoking, your body's oxygen supply improves, leading to increased energy levels and better exercise tolerance. You'll find it easier to engage in physical activities, leading to improved fitness, stamina, and overall well-being.

8. Financial Savings: Smoking is an expensive habit. By quitting smoking, you'll save a significant amount of money that would have been spent on cigarettes. Over time, these savings can add up to substantial amounts, allowing you to invest in other areas of your life.

9. Improved Fertility and Pregnancy Outcomes: Smoking can negatively impact fertility in both men and women. Quitting smoking improves fertility and increases the chances of successful conception. For pregnant women, quitting smoking significantly reduces the risks associated with smoking during pregnancy, such as premature birth, low birth weight, and developmental issues in the baby.

10. Positive Impact on Others: By quitting smoking, you not only improve your own health but also protect those around you from the harmful effects of secondhand smoke. Your decision to quit can inspire others to do the same, creating a healthier environment for everyone.

Quitting smoking is a transformative decision that brings a wide range of physical, emotional, and financial benefits. While the journey may have its challenges, the long-term rewards of improved health and well-being make it well worth the effort.

CHAPTER 6 CONTINUED

-REBUILDING SELF-IMAGE AND CONFIDENCE

Rebuilding self-image and confidence after quitting smoking is an important aspect of the journey towards a smoke-free life. Here's an explanation of how you can work on rebuilding self-image and confidence during this process:

1. Acknowledge Your Accomplishment: Recognize and celebrate the fact that you have made the decision to quit smoking. Understand that quitting smoking is a significant achievement that requires determination and strength. Give yourself credit for taking this positive step towards better health and well-being.

2. Focus on the Positives: Shift your focus towards the positive aspects of quitting smoking. Remind yourself of the numerous benefits you are experiencing or will experience as a result of being smoke-free. This can include improved health, increased energy levels, better physical appearance, and a longer life expectancy. By focusing on the positives, you can reinforce a positive self-image and boost your confidence.

3. Set Small Goals: Setting small, achievable goals along your smoke-free journey can help build your self-image and confidence. Break down the process of quitting smoking into manageable steps and celebrate each milestone reached. For example, you can set goals such as going a certain number of days without smoking, reducing the number of cigarettes smoked per day, or completing a week without any cigarettes. Achieving these goals will reinforce your belief in your ability to overcome challenges.

4. Practice Self-Care: Engage in activities that promote self-care and well-being. Take care of your physical health by exercising regularly, eating nutritious foods, and getting enough rest. Engage in activities that bring you joy and relaxation, such as hobbies, spending time with loved ones, or practicing mindfulness and meditation. Prioritizing self-care sends a message to yourself that you deserve to be taken care of, which can positively impact your self-image and confidence.

CHAPTER 6 CONTINUED

5. Surround Yourself with Support: Seek support from loved ones, friends, or support groups who can provide encouragement and understanding during your journey. Share your successes, challenges, and feelings with them. Having a support network can help you feel understood, validated, and supported, which can aid in rebuilding your self-image and confidence.

6. Positive Affirmations: Use positive affirmations to reframe your mindset and boost your self-image. Repeat positive statements to yourself, such as "I am strong," "I am in control of my choices," or "I am proud of myself for quitting smoking." By consistently reinforcing positive beliefs about yourself, you can enhance your self-image and confidence.

7. Learn from Relapses: If you experience a relapse or slip-up during your journey to quit smoking, it's important to be kind to yourself and view it as a learning opportunity. Instead of dwelling on feelings of guilt or failure, identify the triggers or situations that led to the relapse and develop strategies to cope with them in the future. Recognize that quitting smoking is a process, and setbacks are a normal part of the journey. By learning from relapses, you can strengthen your resilience and confidence in your ability to overcome challenges.

8. Seek Professional Help if Needed: If you find that rebuilding your self-image and confidence is challenging, consider seeking professional help. A therapist or counselor can provide guidance, support, and techniques to help you address any underlying issues that may be impacting your self-image. They can also assist you in developing strategies to rebuild your confidence and maintain a positive mindset throughout your smoke-free journey.

Remember that rebuilding self-image and confidence is a gradual process. Be patient with yourself and practice self-compassion. Over time, as you continue to embrace a smoke-free lifestyle and adopt positive habits, you will find that your self-image and confidence naturally grow.

CHAPTER 6 CONTINUED

–SETTING NEW GOALS AND ASPIRATION

Setting new goals and aspirations when quitting smoking can provide a sense of purpose and motivation throughout your journey. Here's an explanation of how you can approach setting new goals and aspirations:

1. Health and Well-being Goals: One of the most common motivations for quitting smoking is to improve your health. Set specific health-related goals that you want to achieve after quitting smoking. For example, you might aim to improve your lung function, increase your physical fitness, or reduce your risk of developing certain diseases. These goals can serve as a reminder of the positive impact quitting smoking has on your overall well-being.

2. Financial Goals: Smoking can be an expensive habit, and quitting can lead to significant cost savings. Consider setting financial goals with the money you will save by not buying cigarettes. You might save up for a vacation, invest in a hobby or activity you enjoy, or put the money towards a long-term financial goal. Having a clear financial objective can provide added motivation and a tangible reward for your efforts.

3. Personal Development Goals: Quitting smoking presents an opportunity for personal growth and self-improvement. Consider setting goals that focus on areas of personal development. For example, you might want to enhance your stress management skills, improve your self-care routine, or develop healthier coping mechanisms. These goals can help you cultivate a healthier and more balanced lifestyle, contributing to your overall well-being.

4. Physical Activity Goals: Engaging in regular physical activity can complement your efforts to quit smoking. Set goals related to physical activity that align with your interests and abilities. This could involve participating in a specific sport or exercise routine, training for an event like a 5K run or a cycling race, or simply aiming to incorporate a certain number of minutes of physical activity into your daily routine. Regular exercise can help manage cravings, reduce stress, and improve your overall health and fitness levels.

5. Social Goals: Quitting smoking often involves making changes to your social environment. Set goals that focus on developing and nurturing relationships with non-smokers or individuals who support your smoke-free lifestyle. This might involve joining social or recreational groups, connecting with others who have successfully quit smoking, or finding new ways to spend time with friends and loved ones that don't involve smoking. Building a supportive social network can provide encouragement and reinforce your commitment to quitting smoking.

6. Career Goals: Quitting smoking can positively impact your professional life. Use this opportunity to set career-related goals. For instance, you might aim to improve your productivity, enhance your focus and concentration, or seek new opportunities for growth and advancement in your job. By focusing on your professional development, you can channel your energy into building a successful and fulfilling career.

When setting goals and aspirations, ensure they are realistic, specific, and measurable. Break them down into smaller milestones that you can track and celebrate along the way. Also, remember that everyone's journey is unique, so set goals that are meaningful to you personally and align with your values and aspirations.

Regularly revisit your goals, assess your progress, and make adjustments as needed. Celebrate your achievements, no matter how small, and use any setbacks as opportunities for learning and growth. By setting new goals and aspirations on your smoke-free journey, you can maintain focus, maintain motivation, and experience a greater sense of fulfillment and purpose in your life.

CHAPTER 6 CONTINUED

–INSPIRING OTHERS AND GIVING BACK

Inspiring others and giving back when quitting smoking can have a profound positive impact on both yourself and those around you. Here's an explanation of how you can inspire others and give back during your journey to quit smoking:

1. Lead by Example: One of the most powerful ways to inspire others is by demonstrating your commitment to quitting smoking through your actions. As you successfully navigate the challenges of quitting smoking, others who may be struggling with the same addiction can see firsthand that it's possible to overcome it. Your perseverance, determination, and success can serve as a source of inspiration and motivation for others to embark on their own smoke-free journey.

2. Share Your Story: Openly sharing your personal experiences, challenges, and triumphs with quitting smoking can be incredibly inspiring to others. By sharing your story, you create a sense of connection and empathy, letting others know they are not alone in their struggles. Discuss the reasons behind your decision to quit, the difficulties you faced, and the strategies that helped you stay smoke-free. Your authenticity and vulnerability can inspire others to take action and make positive changes in their own lives.

3. Offer Support and Encouragement: As someone who has experienced the challenges of quitting smoking, you can offer support and encouragement to others who are on a similar journey. Reach out to individuals who express a desire to quit smoking and offer a listening ear, share resources and strategies that worked for you, and provide words of encouragement. Your support can make a significant difference in someone's motivation and belief in their ability to quit smoking.

4. Participate in Support Groups: Joining or facilitating support groups for individuals trying to quit smoking can provide an invaluable platform for sharing experiences, offering guidance, and fostering a sense of community. By actively engaging in these groups, you can inspire others through your presence, insights, and support. Hearing stories of success and learning from collective experiences can motivate others to continue their efforts to quit smoking.

CHAPTER 6 CONTINUED

5. Advocate for Smoke-Free Policies: Use your experience and knowledge to advocate for smoke-free policies in your community, workplace, or public spaces. By actively participating in advocacy efforts, such as supporting campaigns, signing petitions, or attending community meetings, you can contribute to creating a healthier environment for everyone. Your advocacy can inspire others to take action and raise awareness about the importance of a smoke-free environment.

6. Volunteer for Smoking Cessation Programs: Consider volunteering your time and expertise with organizations or programs that focus on smoking cessation. You can assist in workshops, support group sessions, or helplines dedicated to helping individuals quit smoking. Sharing your own journey and providing guidance can be a source of inspiration and support for those seeking to quit smoking.

7. Be an Accountability Partner: Offer to be an accountability partner for someone who is trying to quit smoking. This involves providing ongoing support, checking in regularly, and helping them stay motivated and focused on their goals. By offering accountability and encouragement, you can inspire them to push through challenges and remain committed to quitting smoking.

8. Celebrate Milestones: When you or others reach important milestones in your smoke-free journey, celebrate them! Acknowledge and recognize the progress made, whether it's a day, a week, a month, or a year without smoking. Celebrating milestones not only boosts your own motivation and confidence but also inspires others by demonstrating that quitting smoking is achievable and worth celebrating.

Remember, inspiring others and giving back is a continuous process. By sharing your experiences, offering support, and actively participating in efforts to promote smoke-free living, you can positively impact the lives of others and create a ripple effect of inspiration and positive change.

Conclusion

Quitting smoking is a process that requires commitment, perseverance, and support. It's important to set realistic goals, celebrate milestones, and practice self-care throughout the journey. Remember that setbacks may occur, but learning from them and staying focused on your smoke-free future will lead to long-term success and a healthier, happier life.

By choosing a smoke-free future, you prioritize your health, well-being, and personal growth while inspiring and positively impacting others. Embrace the possibilities and opportunities that come with a smoke-free life, and look forward to a brighter and healthier future ahead.

.
Your Smoke-Free Future.

Resource for further assistance:

The easy way to stop smoking" by Allen Carr.